1

Disclaimer:

This book is not perfect; it is not all encompassing in its scope of the "Christian" life. It may not be accepted or acceptable by all of the people in it's intended audience. It is not necessarily spelling out groundbreaking or new ideas about Jesus, and discipleship, and the author is not always consistent or disciplined. This short book is also not meant to criticize without solution or teach without experience. This is my honest dream of the beginning of discipleship life. This is my life and friendship with Jesus Christ, and whether you agree with what I have to say or not, this is part of what I believe God is doing in my Generation. He is so capable that he is using my glaring immaturity and imperfection to display the glory of His perfection in relationship. Please read with an open mind and practice what is written. It might not change your life in relationship with God or your relationship with yourself and the world around you. But it just might.

Please understand.... I love my King and I am out to destroy any and every religious crutch that stands in the way of true friendship.

RELIGIO-CIDE

A Primer on Dismantling the Current Religious Structure for the Sake of True Relationship

By

Tommy Green

The Introduction

Before we begin....

Lord Jesus, You died for my sins and rose again in defiance of death. You did this for all of mankind. You did this for me. Thank You for your mercy and forgiveness. Thank You for dying the way you did for me. Please fill my human spirit with Your Holy Spirit. Please forgive me for all the times I have hurt others and hurt myself and missed the mark. Thank You for Your love. Please let my old life fade away and give me a new life today. Introduce Yourself to me today. Thank You for hearing and answering my prayers. Please God be good to me. Holy Spirit- I am Yours. . . .

Chapter 1. Sin Management = A Designated Driver

I have something to say to every truehearted disciple of Jesus, old or young, newborn or mature, who has bought into the system of self-focused sin management and behavior watching. This mindset is what has entrapped so many people in a cycle of defeat and frustration. It is what we seem to teach and model in church. I don't even really think that the model we have for church is either manageable or fun. But apparently it is all we have. We seem to think that if we take care of the symptoms, we have cured the problem, and that is victory.   If you don't sin then you win. This is not the model of existence we see Jesus Christ give to His disciples in the Gospels.

We, in the church, still live like we have no idea what we are made for, we have no high vision for the Kingdom that Jesus talked about, and we never actually get to believe in our own regeneration fully and completely. Like a drunk driver we say, " I made it home okay and in one piece, I didn't hurt anyone too badly. That counts for something, right?"

We in the body of Christ tend to live in reality like the best we can hope for is to get "saved" by the skin of your teeth and just manage your garbage for long enough to die and go to heaven. Whoopeeee! You did it....

Yeah, I'm sure that is exactly the type of thinking He wanted us to have when Jesus crushed the head of the serpent on our behalf. Destroying the work of the enemy means we don't look at porn anymore, and we don't swear, lie, steal, or chase women. We "Behave." That may or may not have anything to do with actually being friends with Jesus, but we sure "Look" like Christians and as long as we don't commit huge sins all the time, we may make it out of this thing in good shape.

Yep, that was what He was talking about when He said the kingdom of heaven is at hand. Jesus never really meant for us to heal the sick, to raise the dead, to cast out demons, to cleanse the lepers, to preach good news to the poor, or to declare the remission of sins. No, He didn't mean for us to do anything like that when He told us that "as the Father sent me, I send you, and YOU WILL FIGHT

AND WIN." He meant, "Now guys mostly watch your language and stop all that darn sinning."

Sin management, to me, is not what Jesus came to teach us. The lifestyle of sin management teaches, and is primarily focused on, restraining our indulgences and making sure that we are on our best behavior for God and man. That seems to me to be a really gross and fear-based way of walking out what should be freedom. The Lord is Spirit, and where the Spirit of the Lord is, there is FREEDOM. Sin management teaches us that the transformation and power of Jesus working on our behalf can't be trusted past the cross. What kind of power is that? What kind of Christianity and discipleship is that? That does not represent Jesus to the world.

Our sin seems to be so powerful that it even carries with it the power to sway the heart of the Lover of all humanity in heaven. Sin-focused Christianity teaches by definition that our behavior is more powerful than Christ's sacrifice, and has some sort of crazy authority over the love of God. That sounds more like hell than heaven to me.

Romans says nothing created or uncreated can "separate us from the love of God through Christ Jesus our Lord." Get that? Nothing created, nothing uncreated, **nothing** can separate us from His love and acceptance and grace and hope and vision. Jesus is continually releasing and speaking for us in the heavenlies. He lives forever making intercession for us; He sits at the right hand of the Father on our behalf even now, says Romans and Hebrews. And He is longing to see us rise up in victory, of course over our sins and temptation, but not only or even I dare say, primarily that.

Jesus has given us in His word a vision of a Kingdom. He calls us children, kings and priests, He says we are His temple, and He says that He lives on the inside of us now. He has given us such awesome authority and power. He has said that we will defy impossibility. He has said we will do greater things than He did! God is on our side and has such a huge vision for the victory entrusted to us, yet we have reduced the

Gospel of the Kingdom to a doctrine and lifestyle of behavior modification and sin-focused sin management.

So much of the teaching and culture of our church is concerned only with behavior modification as the way to present Jesus to the rest of the world. Now our behavior is addressed in the word of God, and it is important that if our relationship and devotion is real, we allow Jesus to transform us in relationship. But that doesn't mean gritting our teeth in self-discipline and calling it genuine transformation and freedom. We are called to become intimate friends, partners, and disciples of our Master, allowing Him to work on the areas in our lives that will bring true change to our understanding of God and ourselves. We are called to model relationship with Him to the world. That's what the world is going to rest in—relationship—not the structure and culture of "Christianity." Jesus is real and personal, and He can transform us into His image as we behold Him with our faces bare and with nothing to lean on except Him.

The problem is that most people aren't really interested in looking like Jesus. It would appear that our definition of victory in Jesus is simply this: not sinning. That's it? That's the victory of Christ in us? I just don't sin anymore? Wow.

What is your personal definition of salvation? What does it all mean?

I believe in salvation. I believe that we walk in victory over very real enemies as kids in the kingdom of our Father in heaven. But simply not sinning is only one part of salvation. It is true that that we need to continue to walk in a way that honors the sacrifice and gift of Jesus. We need to guard against falling into temptation and living in blatant rebellion or hidden sin before the Father. These things are absolutely necessary and good and right and beautiful to God. However, if this is our entire focus, we make the substance of Christianity and the teaching of what it means to be a Christian a fear-based and sin-focused reaction to the culture around us. That's wrong. We train our brothers and sisters in the body of Christ like we are losing the fight and are on an uphill climb with very little hope. That leads us to believe that the biggest problem with ourselves is how darn powerful our sin is, and how big and bad that enemy guy is who has so much power. That is not thinking or positioning ourselves in line with the will of Jesus for us. That is what makes the church so absolutely ineffective in showing people victory.

I have no reservation in saying that a majority of us in the body of Christ have, on some level, turned the doctrine of grace into a pharisaical exercise in religious manipulation. We have sacrificed the gift of unconditional love, redemption, unlimited freedom and goodness, which is to be prized above all things, for the sake of safety, comfort, and religiously based control.

It is my belief that we have sacrificed the ability to walk in freedom as sons and daughters of GOD for a second-rate, Sunday school, "Christian" experience. We look nothing like Jesus, yet we are careful to produce a weak justification for our lack of revelation, intimacy, power, and relationship face to face with God. We are not free! We are not radical!

We are not REPRESENTING JESUS! While a world is living in hell, we lack the theology sufficient to empower the BRIDE OF JESUS to do anything about it!

Thus begins the exercise: we need to now attempt to establish a real friendship and connection with, and subsequently become like Jesus Christ. You and I as Redeemed mankind need to seek to literally be transformed into the spitting image of God's Son and our Bridegroom, Judge, and King. He was sent to show us the way and to give us the keys. It is time for us to take them, to unlock the door, and to run in the freedom for which He suffered, bled, died, and rose again.

Hebrews 11:3 says that the image of the Father is the Son. This is our destiny as His children: to be made over into His image. Now this does include walking in holiness and righteousness. However, I am convinced we are thinking that holiness and righteousness primarily have to do with our morality. Again I say no, not exactly. Holiness is being, in essence, as God is to the earth: He is higher and other than. His definition is beyond searching out. He is holy. So God says, be like me. That means, of course, to sin no more, sure, but how much more! Really, beloved, can you hear the thoughts of religious performance screaming out, "But we can't sin and be like Jesus. **What about the sin stuff??"** It's true, we should not walk in sin, and most of us try not to. But we do sin, even though our primary motivation at some level is to bring God pleasure with our lives. However, our main motivation and course in life, now that Jesus is with us, cannot focus on being helpless and hopeless in our inferiority and sin. Believe it or not, we are not primarily huge moral failures to God. He knows our hearts, and He has changed our hearts. **The sin stuff was demolished and annihilated once for all on the cross of Christ. Bride of Jesus, rise up and take ground!**

The substance in this piece of reading will not be primarily focused on managing our bad behavior. It will be about teaching us to befriend and become like the One who was so amazing, that in one lifetime, the entire civilized world was turned upside down, and 2000 years later, we can still feel the bomb God dropped on us. That is our legacy as the children of God and the bride of Jesus Christ. We are the Kingdom of Heaven. We are called to live in such a deep and real spiritual friendship with our Father in Heaven, that it transforms not only our individual souls, but touches and reaches the nations of the Earth. The revolution must begin!

Chapter 2. The Remedy is Him: Love

Jesus loves you. Period. You are loved and desired by the God of the whole universe. You do not have to earn His love. God loves you. That is the most important thing in the whole world. You are loved with the type of love you have wanted from the beginning of time. The love that would give anything and everything it had for you, without needing you to do anything in return, is yours. This is the kind of love that truly doesn't need you to do anything to keep the Lover engaged or interested. This love simply exists and takes all of its pleasure in giving itself to you. It is otherworldly to really think about.

Think about all of the people who have loved you or do love you now. Think about what was required to keep that love. Now then, take it a step further. How many people would not give a second thought to dying for you right this moment, if necessary? I'm not talking about dying for you in the heat of the moment, but as a conscious thought, they would not hesitate to give up everything, even their lives, for you. Who would die for you, as if the only reason they were living was to give everything for

you at any moment. How long is the list? Really?
The love we dream of and try to create for ourselves
in relationships is modeled to all mankind in the life
of Jesus Christ.

It is a rare thing to think about this sacrificial
love. In Romans, it basically says this: rarely do you
hear about someone laying down their life for
someone else. And if you laid your life down, it
might be for someone really good; but you don't die
for bad people. It would seem shocking to anyone
who found themselves in a position where a perfect
stranger would take a death sentence on their behalf,
someone they had never met nor spent any time
with. That degree of abandon and compassion and
sacrifice would have a lasting impact on our souls. I
believe any one of us would remember that
encounter for the rest of our days. We might even
seek to find out more about this person who went
through this experience for us, and we might try to
live like that person out of our response to the
kindness and love shown to us. That's essentially a
picture of the story of Jesus and our response to His
sacrifice.

Now understand this: the love of God simply is. God is love. The essence, and power, the fullness and awesome wonder, and glory, passion, and experience of love exists, and all those same definitions apply to God. God is awesome and whole in Himself. You need to understand that there is nothing that we could add or take away from God. Yet God has made Himself vulnerable to us a Father and Lover and Friend of humanity, which means to you and to me. We are created beings and He is our Creator with the understanding and knowledge of the big picture. This same God just loves you, and He designed you for the sole purpose of expressing His love back to Him and to all of those around you. His love is the strength of any believer's life. And the lack of God's love in someone's life manifests as a consuming and consistent emptiness that plagues them with heaviness, despair, isolation, and loneliness. God's love simply exists for you and for me, and it is passionate and fiery and consuming and jealous and hot! He just desires you to know Him. It has absolutely nothing to do with your performance for God. As a matter of fact, it is because of our performance as humanity on the earth that we ended up in a position of shame, brokenness, despair, and deception. Without the love and grace of God, we live in a place of continual pressure, struggling to perform to earn the affection and acceptance of this world and the people in it.

So the most important principle of your revolutionary relationship is this: Jesus took care of all of the requirements on behalf of all of us so we now stand in the place of freedom, unconditional love, and acceptance in the eyes of God. **The work is done**. God loves you. God wants you to know who He is and what He is like. God wants you to hang out with Him and talk. He wants you to know that life in His presence and with His Spirit in your life is truth, and every other substitute is rooted in deception. So the first and foundational point I want to convey to you is simply this...

God loves you! God does not want you to "do stuff" for Him first, or to understand how bad or how wrong you are. The first thing that we as the church of Jesus need to understand is that we are loved. That means every day, in every circumstance, in every failure, whether we are having a good day or a horrible day, whether we are in church, out of church, dismantling churches or building churches. God loves you. God is love.

You can stop performing to earn the acceptance of the God who already said, "I love you and accept you already. Be my friend. Be my child. Be mine. Stop trying to be something for me to earn something from me." God's greatest gift is His love for us, regardless of our performance. Stop focusing on trying to clean up your act. That's just acting.

The spirit of religion loves to hide within our biblically- and scripturally-minded thought processes. This spirit sneaks out of the shadows of sin into our fear-based subtleties of thought and personal effort. The spirit of religion stands ready to substitute "discipline" for a gift--the "discipline" of working out the removal of sin from within our being, for the gift of the Holy Spirit and the power of God living in us. In Galatians Paul the Apostle told his readers, "you are all being foolish; after beginning with the Spirit, are you now trying to earn something by human effort?"

Think of this story: Jesus was baptized in the Jordan by John the Baptizer. So Jesus gets baptized and the voice of God speaks, saying, "This is my beloved Son. In Him I am well pleased." Quick question for you: how much work and ministry had Jesus done at that point? Really, how many things had Jesus done in His ministry that would prompt God to say that He was pleased with Jesus? We need to look at that for a second. It is not what you can do for God that dictates how God's heart moves towards you. God has not proposed a performance-based and fear-driven relationship. When we look at Jesus, we see that He had only just stepped into the place and destiny designed for Him by the Father. He had just begun the journey, and God accepted and blessed Him for that first step. In front of everyone, Jesus was honored by God! So are we, the minute we take that first step of receiving what God already has for us. We can experience the overwhelming reality of His love and acceptance, which has nothing to do with what we can do. It is a gift.

God was pleased with Jesus. God is just as pleased with us and takes pleasure in our existence. The "work" God wants is that we believe. Believe that God loves you. Jesus asked the Father that the love that the Father has in heaven would be given to us. We stand in His finished plan and should receive, with freedom, that love—Now! No apologies are needed, just gracious acceptance and relational understanding of our responsibility, in love, to honor His gift, because we care.

When will we as disciples and apprentices, made to walk in His ways, be re-created to be holy, to be miracle workers, children, servants, and lovers of God and each other? When will we actually believe? What's it going to take? How can I express this? We do not need another book here. I'm sorry. But let's have it right. <u>Jesus' love and relationship is all we truly need.</u>

Chapter 3. Jesus is the Model

Wake Up Oh Sleeper, Rise From The Dead, And Christ Will Shine On You. Eph. 5:14

It's Destiny Time!

Any of the ideas expressed within this manual are rooted in the biblically supported assumption that in order to accurately understand who God is, our conclusions need to be based solely, and practiced exclusively and completely, on the expression of the character and nature of God the Father in the person of His Son, Jesus Christ. That means, to be a Christian, we base everything on Jesus Christ.

In order to truly carry a biblical New Testament worldview and remain true to the principles of "Christianity," there is no higher revelation or truth. There is no point in discussing what a Christian is apart from an absolute dependence and reliance on Jesus Christ. He is all we need to see. Ever. He is IT. Jesus Christ is all the "theology" we need. He is perfection personified. Anything else is secondary. Everything else is epilogue to His life, His teachings, His miracles, and His instruction to us as the Head and the Foot and the Whole and the Sum of its parts. He is the MODEL. No one and nothing else will ever contain the essence of the God we seek to find in this life on earth. Jesus Christ is all, period. For real.

Anything that is supposed to represent "Christianity" in its purest form is going to be based on Jesus, not on Christian theology about Him or because of Him. Let's be clear: I am not opposed to theological ideas about God. We as humans, with the ability to think and reason about the essence of truth, need to know the difference between truth and error. In regard to "biblical truth," we need to know what is accurately represented consistently in the character and nature of God, and what is inconsistent with God's character and nature. Now to get the most accurate picture of what His character and nature is, we need to study the life of the Son of God.

Who is Jesus Christ our Lord? I agree with those in the body of Christ who say we need theology to help draw lines between who God is, what God is like, and what is very truly demonic wisdom. The demonic would capture the thoughts and ideas of man and appear to be true, all the while leading people further and further away from God (Col. 2:8). We must be careful to avoid the separation of our souls from the truth--Jesus. That separation could subsequently lead us into a world of confusion, pain, and separation from God, which is one definition of hell itself.

Please understand that great men and women of God have paved a way for many of us by giving definition to God-inspired arguments. They have provided to us ideas that refute the deception of the philosophy and wisdom of this age. We, as Christians in this generation, stand in the grace of Jesus as believers because there are those who have carefully explained the life and person of Jesus, documented and proven from scripture, and inspired by the Holy Spirit. Because of these great people, we have gained understanding and now stand in the grace of Jesus, believing with all of our minds, hearts, and souls. I honor the wisdom of God for creating great, thinking men and women who walked through the different stages of the life of the body of Christ. They refuted the unbelievable thievery and manipulation of the gospel of Jesus by our true enemy in the spirit, Satan. His goal, as a thief, a liar, and A DEFEATED FOE, has always been to try to lead people into deception, isolation, and eternal darkness. **We must stand with our forbears, realizing that hell is reserved for Satan and his minions, NOT for God's children. And so we fight.**

Jesus said to His followers, if you have seen Me, then you have seen the Father (John 14:8-9). The first chapter of the letter to the Hebrew people (Hebrews 1:3) says, "He is the radiance of God's glory and the express image of the Fathers being. . . ." This scripture characterizes Jesus as the representation of the total understanding of the Father. He is the express image of who the Father is and what the Father is like. What the Father is like in His heart and compassion and justice and reign in relationship to humanity, is defined in Jesus Christ. Colossians speaks of Jesus as the image of the invisible God (Colossians 1:15). John speaks of Jesus as the incarnate Word of the Father in heaven (John 1:1-2). The essence of the character of the

God whom Christians worship is presented in the life of our resurrected Lord, Master, and Messiah, Jesus Christ (Col. 1:19-20). There is no point in discussing anyone else as a model for Christianity in this written work. We have Jesus.

The reason for taking such a stand on Christ alone is to challenge a new generation of Christians to return to our first Love. FOR REAL. We need to base our relationships and lives on the person of Jesus, in theory and in practice. We cannot base anything on mere ideas, but we must take action to become like Him. The ones who hear and practice need to live, not merely as hearers of the WORD, but doers of Jesus' way and will in the earth. It is a terrifying thing to fall into the hands of the living God, but we are IIis workmanship, created in Christ Jesus to DO WORK ORDAINED BEFORE THE WORLD BEGAN! We have an awesome assignment with our eternal destiny. Our destiny is defined JESUS CHRIST (2 cor. 3:18)! The new kids, men, and women that are coming up need to see Jesus Christ--not great men and women, not wonderful theologians, not fiery preachers, and not the traditions now found in body and bride of Jesus.

I dare say the mess we get ourselves into is this: we sacrifice the freedom of pursuing Jesus, and true transformation, for the traditions of the church. We need Jesus. To coin the phrase of a brother in the Lord, "Jesus Christ is perfect theology."

This short manual I hope becomes a small nudge into the reality of the Kingdom of Heaven. That Kingdom is the Gospel that Jesus preached and commanded his disciples to preach, both before and after He was glorified. This is not about you becoming a normal Christian person. It is not about raising up people to "go to church." It is about you understanding and knowing Jesus as the King, and you knowing and taking your place as a son or daughter of God in the kingdom. You belong in the kingdom, of which you are an heir with Jesus Christ. You are not to be a church disciple, but a kingdom Disciple. God forbid that you settle for anything less than the reality of Jesus Christ in you, the hope of glory-- your hope of glory, and the only hope this world will ever know.

Jesus is the model, and you will become like Him with this life you have been given. We start now. The revolution builds.

Chapter 4.   Following the Leader

He breathed on them and said, "Receive the Holy Spirit. He will be with you and in you. He will guide you in all truth. The world does not know Him, the Counselor and the Spirit of Truth. He will take from me and make it known to you. God has shown us these things by His Spirit." They were baptized with the Holy Spirit and began to prophesy and speak in tongues. . . .

You cannot follow Jesus without an active, living relationship with the Holy Spirit. If this is not a part of your denominational background or understanding, then you need to look at the possibility that your denomination's pursuit of discipleship is possibly unbiblical and in religious error, meaning it is not based on the life of Jesus but on the traditions of man. The potential danger to you is that your experience in relationship with Jesus could be severely compromised in richness and depth because of the religious hindrance in the ideas supported by your current community. It is time that we value the presence and ministry of the Spirit of Truth over church traditions.

This is about KNOWING GOD and being known by God. Jesus says to His disciples in their day, (and to us as His body and disciples in this day), that He is the Good Shepherd and that the sheep know His voice. We are called in the word of God "the sheep of His pasture." We understand from the Psalms that "He leads us in green pastures, and beside still waters." He says that His sheep understand the difference between the true shepherd and the hired hand, who is the liar that cares nothing for the sheep. So we are invited to develop a biblical understanding of the dynamic of relationship and communication between God and us. When we create space and time for Jesus to speak to us individually and corporately, we give God more of an opportunity to anchor us in His desire for us to live in spirit and in truth. We need to understand the truth to which we are called: to know God, and be known by God. This is either a real relationship built on communication, trust, love, and faith in each other, or it is religion. Our only hope is to be bound to ideas and principles about God that we can't fully comprehend while we remain in the presence of God as a daily experience.

How can you know God if you know nothing of the Counselor, the Spirit of Truth? The Spirit is the one who leads us to Jesus, the very Spirit that raised Christ from the dead. He dwells within the redeemed child of God and will bring all things to remembrance at their proper time. **The Holy Spirit is God and is to be honored by every person who calls on the name of Jesus. He is not just as an idea but a person to be called upon in daily practice.**

As a short prayer within this small text, I just want to acknowledge God right now.

"Holy Spirit please come and encounter every reader at this moment. Speak with them and to them. Move in communion within their conscience, within their heart and use whatever means You need to, to make known the truth of who You are to them. Holy Spirit, use Your voice to lead Your people to the resurrected Lord and Savior, Jesus, right now. Thank You. You are honored here."

Everyone can and should hear the voice of Jesus. It is the will of God that you and the Lord develop a relationship and way of communication in the Holy Spirit.

<u>Some Guidelines for Communication</u>:

So here is how we all start. Those who come to God must first believe that He is, and also that He rewards those who seek after Him. Seek and you will find, knock and the door will be opened. The sheep know the voice of the Good Shepherd. **I am telling you God will and can communicate with you in a way that you can understand.** This is not about you listening to me tell you how it is going to happen; that can create major problems. The Holy Spirit of Jesus knows you from before you were born, and knows the best way to encourage you, comfort you, strengthen you, and make you laugh. He can bring about conviction, test your motives, and show you His desires for the world around you. He knows how to build you up and deal with you as a child of God. He can take care of you.

I am asking you to trust God's ability to communicate with you, over your ability to hear from God. God is able to do this in you and for you. Trust him.

God has wonderful things to say to you. He speaks to you as a child, and His heart welcomes you as a loving parent. He sees you as the bride of Jesus prepared for the Bridegroom Himself. He is the Judge who has already ruled and judged in our favor in the person of Jesus, and the King who is already entrusting us with a Kingdom that will never be shaken. He has great love for you, so expect to hear good, encouraging, comforting, and edifying things from the Holy Spirit. Jesus will always speak what is consistent with His character and nature and behavior as shown in the Bible. That being said He may not use language. God's first language isn't language, it's communication: art, songs, poems, sounds, smells, nature, friends, people. God will use all manner of things to communicate with you in a way that will bless you and encourage you in relationship with him. Eternal life is to know Him as He is. Expect God to lead you in a way that will ultimately bring you the greatest level of fulfillment and joy that is deeply rooted in the Spirit of Truth.

Starting Out:

Sit down in a comfortable place that is quiet and restful to your busy soul. Bring a journal, a sketchbook, or an instrument with you if you would like. Spend some time in worship, reading about Jesus and thinking on Him. Sing a bit, if you like. This is all meant to help you set your mind on heavenly things where Christ is seated.

Now this is where it gets really simple. Ask God to speak with you about something. Talk to God. Then wait to hear back from Him. I guarantee you will hear something pop into your mind, a verse will float up, or something in your conscience might be triggered, such as an image from a movie, a verse from a song, or a random thought that might even seem kind of stupid. Don't criticize it or judge it. Take note.

(Disclaimer: Anything that brings condemnation or self hatred, anything that speaks from a place of threatening or demonic energy, anything that contradicts the written word of scripture, or conflicts with what you are understanding is the character and heart of Jesus, our Living Word, anything that you truly do not feel in your spirit is from Jesus, you have

the right and authority as a child of God and under the
authority of the word of Jesus to say, "No." and disregard.
This is about relationship and you will only listen to the voice
of the Good Shepherd. The voice of another we do not listen to
or accept. It is also absolutely biblical and right and healthy
to get counsel from faithful and expectant mentors and friends
in the Lord, if you are having trouble understanding
something you think has been communicated to you. Search
the word of God and seek council if necessary, but do not back
off of this issue in relationship.)

So take note of what showed up. If nothing
happened that minute (or in two or five or twenty),
do not judge or criticize yourself. When we ask of
God, He responds to us. It is that simple. So you
have permission right now to trust that God will
show you something or speak to you about whatever
you just brought up. It may take a while to
understand how God relates and communicates with
you, just for you. **I will say it again, DO NOT
JUDGE OR CRITICIZE YOURSELF if it didn't
happen the way you thought, or if you feel
like it didn't happen at all. That is not the
heart of God for you**.

Take my experience for example. I am a busy, active, hyper-minded kind of guy. Sometimes it takes a little bit of time for me to hear from the Lord. Most times I will realize when I take the pressure off of myself, that I walked away from my time with Jesus with much more than I thought. As soon as I stop freaking out, the seed of faith blossoms in an instant, and I go, "OH! That, that's funny! No, I didn't think that was You. Oh cool. Really?" You will not be disqualified or pushed away by Jesus in this exercise. I bet if you give yourself some grace, you will realize that God communicated something to you in a way that you could understand.

I have seen it countless times. People have thought, "Oh, I got nothing" at first, only to realize two seconds later, "Oh, wait, that showed up and I thought it was just me." Or I just felt peace or calm or something, or perhaps a memory came up or something subtle. That is awesome and okay! Reflect and then test it. It may have been the Lord. You are a child of God and God always has the time to talk with his kids.

The reason this is the most important exercise to begin with is to help you understand that your place and identity is in relationship with God, not with a book or a group of people who claim to be anything. Jesus died to have relationship with you. It is critical in this revolutionary time that we live in, that you develop a love language with the Father--at cost to your entertainment, your other interests, your social life, or whatever takes your time away from God. Get to know the voice of the Father, whatever that is like for you. You have the word of God to back you up and you have the Spirit of Jesus living on the inside of you. The Counselor and Spirit of Truth is with you. Do not be afraid. Know Him! Hear His voice! Make Him known!

How are you supposed to do what He tells you if you don't know how to hear from Jesus? Again, a clear biblical mandate is in place, but there are specific encounters and expressions of the love of God for specific people at specific times and we cannot afford to waste time. This is not one-size-fits-all Christianity and you are not a one-size-fits-all type of disciple.

Understand that listening to God will impact not only you, but as you grow in your ability to listen, He may bring you into the town square to speak a word in season. He may lead you into the darkest parts of the world, or He may lead you to stand before kings and leaders as a testimony. At such times you will be given what you need to say.

This is how we prepare to hear from God each and every day. We learn to do only what we see our Father doing as we are about His business. This is critical for the type of evangelism and outreach needed.

In order to attempt to accurately represent Jesus in this age and in the generation we live in, we are required to walk in the relationship that we profess to the world. To do this, we have to get to know the communication and voice of the Lord. This will not only add and/or begin a wonderful dynamic and understanding in our relationship with Jesus, but it will also prepare us to live out our faith and lead people in the world into relationship, and salvation, found only in our Lord Jesus Christ.

To clarify:

This lesson was merely an exercise in waiting prayer, where we can "be still and know that [He] is God." God will be lifted up and exalted when we spend time with Him. Where there is repentance and rest, there is our victory, and quietness and trust becomes our strength. Sometimes we need to quiet our busy minds and allow God to get busy.

Here ends the lesson.

Chapter 5.   Healing the Sick and Afflicted; On Righteousness

Matthew 6:1 speaks of "acts of righteousness." The word <u>righteous</u> has been used in a number of different ways to support the lifestyle of sin management in Christianity, and it is important to explain the true meaning of the word. The word <u>righteousness</u> is the word <u>tzedekah</u>, which contains in it the idea of our relationship with and expressions of the goodness of God.

We sometimes confuse the definition and meaning of righteousness as being in our theological "position" before the Father, standing in the absolute grace, the completed and finished work of Christ, as sinners saved. Amen to that! That is absolutely true, to a degree. That is a part of it; but again, this definition has had the tendency to focus us on our sin problem, and, subsequently, on our behavior. That is not the fullness of the definition. What I am trying to discuss here is the idea of righteousness as the "stuff" we do to exhibit not only our devotion to God as disciples, but most importantly, the righteousness we display that expresses God's heart and nature to the world.

You DO righteousness to show people how good God is. Righteousness is showing people goodness and mercy and justice and equity and love. Our "acts of righteousness" are primarily what I am discussing. In Revelation this is described as our "linen pure and white," the stuff made of our acts in the name of the Father to demonstrate His character and nature. This is the word tzedekah: the things we do in relationship to communities to demonstrate His righteousness in the midst of an unrighteous world. We stand as sons of God, sanctified unto Him and showing world the righteousness of God. We overcome that which stands in opposition to the Lord, by His righteous deeds done through us and in us. That is righteousness. That is where I am coming from as I continue. This is practical righteousness: not only ministering to the poor and the hungry but also to the sick, the dying, the hurting, and the demonically oppressed (Isaiah 61 style!).

Jesus made some really simple commands when He walked the earth. Exhibiting the true character and nature of the Father He knew so well was the core of his ministry. He brought the Father glory and He instructed His disciples to follow His lead. "As the Father sent me, so I send you."

Now understand this, in the span of one human lifetime, Jesus exhibited to mankind the complete and total understanding of who God is (Hebrews 1:3). This is how He showed us how God feels towards the earth. "The kingdom of heaven is near. Heal the sick. Raise the dead. Cast out demons and cleanse the lepers. Freely you have received, so freely give." To express the heart of God to the generation and nations that were in His sphere of influence, Jesus healed all the sick and demonized individuals who came to Him. He did not turn anyone away. NO ONE WENT AWAY SICK. THIS IS OUR EXAMPLE. Biblically this is the standard.

The greatest model we can follow and emulate is the man Jesus Christ. Jesus is the model--not your church, not your pastor, not anyone else. Jesus is your model for being a "Christian." So, based on Jesus' life and ministry in representing the heart of God to mankind, what can we say about your role in participating in the ministry of physical healing and release from demonic oppression? Answer: EVERY CHRISTIAN HAS THE RESPONSIBILTY AND HONOR TO HEAL THE SICK AND SET THE CAPTIVE FREE TO BRING GLORY TO JESUS.

You cannot find one recorded instance in the Bible where Jesus showed up, someone said "I am sick," and Jesus said, "I cannot help you because it is not the will of the Father." I will buy you an ice cream if you can. I will also be excited to see what Bible you read because that never happens in the Gospels. There is not one recorded incident where someone asks Jesus for healing and he says "Nope," and that person goes away without Jesus healing them. Jesus healed ALL who came to him. Everyone who came to him was HEALED.

When Jesus healed Peter's mom and a bunch of other people at her door, the Bible goes on to say this was to fulfill what was written in Isaiah: "He carried our infirmities and bore our diseases."

By His stripes ALL ARE HEALED. We do not have any excuses; there is no other option. This does not mean that every person I pray for is healed. It makes more sense biblically to believe that whether healing occurs or not is a matter of faith or agreement, or lack of faith, or perhaps demonic strongholds in us that are rooted in deception. It is possible that our failures in healing are the result of own stupidity and bad choices. But, based on the example of Jesus, I cannot take the position that it is not the will or desire of God to heal. To say it was not God's will to heal a person is a doctrine based more on my own disappointment when things don't work out, than on a doctrine based on the testimony and life of Jesus.

If I look at Jesus, everyone who came to Him was healed. He would not dominate the will of people without faith in a region or a community, but the ones who came were ALL healed. If someone comes to me to be healed, my model is Jesus. He did it, and I will believe for the same results that He had and said I should have. I cannot back off of the issue and try to make up excuses for my lack of authority and power over healing in the name of Jesus.

Hear me on this as well. I do not presently see everyone I pray for healed. Get that? But my model does not change, since Jesus does not change. I continue to believe that those results and disappointments have more to do with my earthly circumstances and opposition from the enemy than it does with a God who has already sent His perfect Son to carry all infirmity and disease, along with all sin and death, to the cross with Him. My failure to heal others is more on me as a disciple, and the understanding and revelation I can walk in as I minister to those in need. My failures may be in the way I go about it, but it is not about God's will in the matter. God's will was exemplified in the life of Jesus. His will is made plain to us when it comes to the sick and the dying; what would Jesus do? He healed ALL who came to him. So now it is up to me to continue to believe that everyone I pray for will be healed. It is His will to heal the sick. He healed everyone who asked him. That is my example and it should be yours as well when it comes to a sick and dying world. Your example is Jesus' life--not your church's doctrine, not someone else's theology, or your own failed experiences. <u>Jesus is the highest and best example</u>. So as we continue, and as we walk in faith, we will see more people healed as we pray for more people. We cannot and should not stop.

So understand, Jesus commanded us to heal the sick and set captives free. We need to continue to press on to the goal that Jesus set for us and also we need to continue to believe that Jesus said we should walk like Him if we claim to live in Him. In regards to healing and deliverance, there is no difference in the distinction. Jesus healed and delivered, so I do, and so should we all. There is no other way of being a true disciple of Jesus except to believe and pursue the type of absolutely overflowing love, generosity, and healing power that Jesus had. You cannot be a biblical disciple of Jesus and not desire to live and walk in every way like the Master.

If we, as the bride and body of Christ, start dividing the ministry of Jesus into denominational boxes, we risk the same accusation issued to the Corinthians by Paul the Apostle: "Was Jesus divided? Are you followers of the men who lead you or Jesus himself?" Too often the church has become mired in the doctrine of men. This is the state of many of our body. It cannot remain this way for long. The sea of human need is beckoning us to step out of our man-made boats, contraptions, and props, so we can walk on water to meet them. It is our call to display God's goodness to all we encounter who are sick and under oppression, that we, by the power of Christ, will transform them with the healing and deliverance of our resurrected Lord. Jesus desires us to do what He does and to be like Him in every way possible, representing Him to the people in this world each and everyday.

Exercise:

Pray for someone who is sick or in pain. Make sure you are not standing at some religious distance from them as people. It is all about demonstrating the love of God, not you being a superhero. Take a moment to connect with God in prayer. Listen for His instruction on how to proceed. Then declare in intercession whatever God lays on your heart and watch the power of sickness, and sin, and death be broken off of them as you believe they will walk away free. This exercise will help you understand and do the work that Jesus did:

to display the righteousness of God to this situation and circumstance.

Let it be recorded in the book of Heaven that at this moment we stood up and said "No" to the work of hell, and Jesus saw our faith and met it with his power in us and healed the infirm.

The Bible as foundation:

The following scriptures lay a foundation for us as we persist in healing:

- Psalm 103:1-6—God heals ALL.

- Isaiah 53:1-6—By his stripes we are healed.

- Mark 2:1-12—Forgiveness of sins is His ultimate healing. He gives us authority in healing.

- Mark 5:1-43—Deliverance, death, and power going out.

- Mark 7:24-30—Honoring desperation.

- Mark 8:22-26—Pray more than once.

- Mark 9:14-30—Prayer and fasting.

- Mark 16:6—The victory for all of us His supremacy as Lord.

- Mark 16:9-20—Our journey.

Tips for praying for those that are demonized:

Praying for people that are afflicted with any demonic bondage, affliction, or oppression is healing prayer as well. We are healing wounded bodies, wounded souls, and wounded spirits in the name and authority that is in Jesus. Jesus has all authority in heaven and on earth. Speak this out. We are not to be afraid and intimidated by the demonic realm. We also are not to make a game of this. It is not a light thing. Demonic spiritual affliction and oppression is very real and its symptoms can appear quickly and in many different forms. If you hear or feel in the Spirit that there is demonic influence in a situation, here are some good steps to pray through with the person.

Demonic influences can manifest as shame, depression, despair, suicide, murder, control, manipulation, lust, pride, envy, lies, rage, malice, rejection, religion, hatred, and fear. Be aware.

Command all demonic influence to be silenced in the name of Jesus. They are not allowed to shout or interrupt in anyway. They are not allowed to show boat like it's a scene a horror movie or something. You stand as a minister of the healing of Jesus. You stand as one with the authority of Jesus Christ in your life. He holds the keys and we speak His authority over the situation quickly. They are not allowed to act like they are bigger than Jesus. They are not. Do not be afraid.

Again, this is not a horror movie. While the horror is real, this is one of God's children, and they need healing and freedom now. This is not a time for games and hesitation; quickly speak the authority of the blood of Jesus and the resurrection of Jesus over the person. If you can get them to pray a prayer of forgiveness for any of the spiritual doors they may have opened into the demonic world, this is good. Lack of forgiveness, bitterness, and hatred towards others can open up powerful doors and footholds for the enemy to operate in the life of people, so forgiveness is always healing to the whole person. Ask them to pray in the name of Jesus, and if there is strong demonic opposition, then command release from demonic affliction in Jesus name.

If you can lead them in a time of communion with you, make a table for the Lord's Supper, asking them to spend some time expressing repentance and asking for the body and blood of Jesus to be represented in their life. You will most likely deal with a host of issues, emotionally and spiritually, as well as physically, and lead them into a time of fuller restoration and healing in the long run.

Continue to pray until the breakthrough comes. If the person is not willing to receive healing or is too connected with the doors they may have opened, or demonic power they enjoy feeling--well, in short, they don't want to let go of what is afflicting them. You may stand at an impasse. If they don't want to be free, you can't do it for them. Personally, you and your group may need to pray and fast for future encounters in prayer and healing to be successful with such a person. This can be tricky stuff, and I have experience, but I am not a master at understanding the realm of darkness. I choose instead to focus on the King and the Kingdom of Light, which is superior to realm of darkness where the demonic kingdom derives its power and authority.

You are always allowed to ask for council and seek help from people with a greater understanding, experience, and wisdom than you possess within the body of Christ. You do not have to "go it alone" and it is best if you don't. Please seek responsible shepherds, pastors, and leaders that can help you come into a deeper maturity and understanding about the spiritual realm and the work of hell in people's lives. These are simply tips that I have gathered in years of ministry and gleaned from others with more understanding than myself.

Total healing for soul and body is ours in the life and death and resurrection of Jesus. Press in. Don't be unaware of or overly spooked by demonic influence. God will let you know. This is not meant to be spooky or crazy stuff; while demons are real, Jesus really has authority over them all.

He wins, and we win in his victory. This is another face of salvation in Christ.

<u>Tips for ministering to those who are sick, diseased, or in pain:</u>

Think of pain as being on a scale of 0-10. If someone has a pain level that they categorize as a 10, pray until it goes down to a 0. Do not be afraid to persist in prayer over and over again until the change comes and it breaks into their experience. If they took aspirin and their pain level went down, they would rejoice, so steal that thunder before they take the pill, and bomb 'em with the healing power of God, giving the glory to Jesus! Ask them if they are in pain. If so, ask how it feels on the scale of 0-10, then ask to pray and declare the pain broken in the name of Jesus. Do whatever God wants you to do, and watch. Ask the person if they are any better, any worse, or if there is no change. Let them be honest with you. Do not be afraid that it is not working. Prayer is powerful and it always does something in the spirit.

Pain reduction is a manifestation of the healing of Jesus. Also, pursuing healing in this way is one of many ways to get used to praying for the sick and seeing them recover.

Praying for miracles will manifest in different ways. Sometimes it is instantaneous, other times it takes place within a few minutes, or longer. Sometimes in the process of praying for one thing, God just touches a completely different area. All of a sudden the person is healed of some affliction and begins to praise GOD, or sits in disbelief, or freaks out all together.

Personal Testimony:

I prayed for a lady that was deaf in her left ear. She had no hearing at all, and after operations, still nothing. She approached me and said, " I don't want to be deaf anymore." Talk about a set up. Geez, it was like she had the faith of the women in the Bible who show up and said, "HELP ME." So I placed my hand on her ear and commanded healing in the name of Jesus. All of a sudden I could literally feel the heat and movement of the Holy Spirit in my hand. I am hyperactive and sort of absent-minded, and not the most "spiritually sensitive" person around, but I just knew that something was happening in my body and in hers as I prayed. I stopped speaking out loud, and, because I wasn't sure if she was a Christian or not, I said, "I'm not, not praying. I'm just hanging out 'cause it really feels like God is doing something and I can feel Him healing your ear. So I'm just going to hang out and chill with God until. . ." "I can hear you," she interrupted, and I freaked out! It was nuts! I was aware of what was going on, so I just gave praise to Jesus and asked her to describe what was happening.

She began rubbing her fingers together near her ear and she cried when the soft and subtle sound of her fingers rubbing together hit her now- healed eardrum. She had friends whisper in her ear and then she repeated what they had said. She also cried as she told us about working retail at the mall, and that now she wouldn't have to listen out of one side of her head and say "WHAT??" all the time to customers. The simple things were becoming simple again, and she wept and cried with her friends that had come.

Most of the kids at the Bible study who witnessed the healing of that lady's ear had never seen anything like that before, and they sat in shock. But now they are used to seeing the power of God time and time again in an atmosphere of belief in God's power and authority. Healing is a part of their reality as they are settling into their discipleship in Jesus now. These are young high school age kids, and they now operate in the same way. Miracles happen, and we can partner with the Miracle Worker to become miracle workers in His name. Like Jesus said to His disciples when the kid showed up with his lunch and they needed to feed thousands: I will bless it and you give them something.

Chapter 6. Living in the Written Word

This is the chapter where we talk about the written word of God and its absolute, uncompromising necessity in understanding the character and nature of God, as well as in understanding and discerning the realities of the natural and supernatural world. If you want to understand Jesus, you need to go to the historical data and to the story of what He says about Himself, making this your basis for seeing who Jesus is. In His life as a human, He showed us who the Father is.

The written word of God is the clearest, easiest, and best way for Jesus to speak. He will communicate all the time in a multitude of ways, but we must look to God's written word to determine if what we think we have heard is truly from God.

We all should seek to commune with God in fun, interesting, and creative ways, but we should always check what we think we have heard against the written word. So, in framing and underscoring the absolute necessity of relationship that is experiential with Jesus, we cannot move forward without speaking to the issue of deception in the earth and the principle of spirit and truth in the kingdom. There is never a higher prophetic word or standard by which we live our lives. We must not be afraid of God speaking stuff to us that blows our minds, challenges our ideas of Him, and stretches our understanding and concepts. But we must remember that scripture says:

- Let God be true and every man a liar.

- Sanctify them by Your truth Father; Your word is truth.

- You diligently study the scriptures because you think that by them you possess life. These are the scriptures that speak of Me, yet you refuse to come to Me to have life.

- Your word is a lamp to my feet and a light to my path.

- RENEW YOUR MIND by the Spirit of God and the word of truth.

There are tons of different ideas about Jesus. Some are rooted in biblical truth, and some are absolutely conjured in the minds of men. Some are demonically inspired to seem like wisdom, but have no basis in the realities of what Jesus has presented of himself. All of us at some point or another have been persuaded to believe certain things about Jesus, and most of us, when we come into relationship with Jesus, begin to have some of those ideas changes--ideas about life and ourselves and God and death and future and pleasure and love.

The process of allowing God to be God in our understanding is a PROCESS. This is true "repentance," where God is allowed to change our thinking about something. True repentance changes our minds, which will result in a changes in us, be it our direction, our goals, or simply our beliefs or ideas. **In order for the process to come into a place of health and truth, it needs to be rooted and grounded in the truth that God has provided for us in his word. That may not be where we have gotten our truth in the past, but that is where the ultimate truth rests, with God and in his wisdom.**

He has given us wisdom, instruction, and guidelines for understanding who He is, who we are, and what our role is to be in these short days we are given to live. **The guide is the Holy Spirit and the instruction manual is the holy written word of God called the BIBLE. This is now your standard.**

In order for our minds to be renewed, we need what a dear spiritual mentor has called, "the two catalysts for freedom--spirit and truth." The Holy Spirit provides the spiritual dynamic to our experience, and the Word of God is the standard of truth. In order to worship and adore God in accordance with His honest heart, we need to worship Him in spirit and truth. **We stand in agreement with what He says about Himself to better grow in conviction about Him. We do this by understanding and searching out what He has said in the Bible**. Standing with Him in His word, allowing His word to speak forth, is one dynamic of what is called intercession: standing in the gap and allowing the Word of God, Jesus, to work in the experience of those who hear it. Faith comes by hearing the word of God.

Jesus states in John that the word of the Father IS Truth. The Spirit of Jesus revealing himself in the BIBLE IS the way that we come into an understanding of the full nature of the truth of the Word of God, living and written, or breathed on this side of eternity. The Bible is the written instruction designed by the Lord to reveal who He is. That is the standard for our knowledge of the testimony of God the Father, God the Son, and God the Holy Spirit. A passion and zeal for understanding, revelation, and knowledge of the written word of God is absolutely essential for anyone wishing to develop a relationship based in the truth of Jesus himself. We all need to stay HUNGRY for the truth to be found in the Bible.

It's easy to come up with stories and ideas about the Son of God that are popular or rooted in an agenda of the antichrist spirit in the earth. That spirit seeks to portray Jesus as someone other than who HE portrayed HIMSELF to be, namely God the Son. He said He is one with the Father, the I AM. He did not describe Himself as just a good teacher, or a powerful prophet, or some sweet dude that showed us how to be good humans. Jesus said He is actually GOD. That is critical and **the more time you take to understand who Jesus is in the Bible, the more of a grid you will have to discern truth from error in life.** The reality of what I'm saying is that once you develop a relationship with Jesus in its seed stages, the biblical framework will guide you, in partnership with the Holy Spirit, coming into a mature and deeply organic relationship for life with the everlasting and eternal God.

I would desire for you that the Bible becomes the most important piece of literature you can own and study for the remainder of your life. That is not to the exclusion of all other writings, but the Bible is the story of Jesus. Get it and devour it. There are numerous written works that will shed light on the holy writings we now have in the Bible, but there is only one completely divinely inspired work, and that is the written word of God. You will be challenged in your trust of the book, but in order for your mind to be renewed in the spirit of Jesus, you need to apply your life to Jesus' heart and mind as seen in the word of truth, the Bible. The Bible needs to become your second language, or even your first language. Either way, what I'm driving at is this: get the book and read it everyday until you have Jesus so burned on your heart and mind and will and emotions, that when you read of Jesus, you see the heart of God the Father. Keep the words and stories of the ministry Jesus burning in your heart, and the Holy Spirit will guide you to such a deep understanding that you will weep openly. My prayer for you is that you will be led into a deeper level of intimacy with Jesus by the Holy Spirit through the word of truth as you read this incredible book.

Tips:

Here are some tips for you to make Bible study easier for you.

1. Get involved in a local weekly Bible study group that is a comfortable place for you to develop your understanding of the word of God. My hope is that you would devote yourself to understanding Jesus' heart, mission, and life, allowing God to so shape and renew your mindset that the wisdom of Jesus would rest with you. Then you would

move into a place where you could lead a group into relationship with Jesus. I want you to become someone who helps guide the next group of people that don't know Jesus into full relationship with Him. The end goal is, by deepening your own relationship with Jesus, you become able to help other people to experience a real relationship with Jesus as well. Get into it!!!!

2. Find a version of the Bible that you understand. Some are easier to read than others. Buy the one that suits your ability to understand and GET IT with a smile. Read several versions, and then pick the one that allows you to say, "I get it. I get that one."

3. Before you read a passage or chapter, say a quick prayer, asking that the Holy Spirit make Jesus known to you. Ask that for help in increasing your understanding so that you will see what it is that God needs you to see. Take a second and just acknowledge that without God, you may just see words on a page, but with His Spirit moving within you

and leading you, you can truly encounter
Jesus.

4. Keep a journal with your Bible just because a
    lot of times you will have thoughts, ideas, and
    stories that stick with you. Allow God to help
    you keep track of what you are discovering.
    Write a commentary of your own; that way
    you will have fun with what the Spirit of Jesus
    shows you. Write or draw the truths you
    discover. Keep that journal so you can
    develop a track record of what God has shown
    you as you have searched out his word.

5. Take your time in reading and thinking about
    what the words mean. Allow God to highlight
    important ideas for you. You'll know what I
    mean when you see it. This is the most
    important reading time you will ever get. This
    is when you as a human have a chance to read
    a story God has inspired men to write down
    through the ages, specifically for YOU--His
    heart to yours. Allow God to talk to you and
    deal with your questions and fears. He can
    provide the answers for whatever pops up.

The word of God is living and ACTIVE. It is divisive, and it will mess with you and help dissect your thoughts about yourself, about others, and most importantly about who God is to you. Let the Word of God do what God wants it to do in the Holy Spirit.

6. Start with the New Testament writings of Jesus, and let that direct you through the Bible. Where there are notes referencing other sections of the Bible, go there and study it up. Let the Bible interpret the Bible. Also read the Psalms and Proverbs like poetry as much as possible. They are awesome!!!!

7. When you don't understand, get good council from a person with wisdom and understanding, someone who is a respectable shepherd or leader in your community. Don't be afraid to ask questions. God is never scared of your questions; God has heard them all.

8. The Bible is complex and written by many writers, so understand that different parts are written different ways. Some of it can be

confusing for a time. Persist and don't get down on yourself if you don't understand something.   Just continue to seek and you will gain understanding from the Lord. Remember that He has also given you vast resources in the forms of people, literature, classes, schools, and the Web to help you discover answers to your questions. You can find the answers; just make sure you ask the Lord to direct you when you are confused.

Chapter 7.   Atmosphere Your Great Ally: On Waiting Prayer

One of the things we see in the life of Jesus that is important for us to acknowledge and learn about is the closeness of His relationship with the Father. Because of that dynamic connection and relationship that was so deeply spiritually powerful, there was a specific atmosphere that Jesus carried and created wherever He went. Jesus carried the tangible presence of heaven with Him wherever He went. He lived in a place of total dependence and understanding of the goodness and love of the Father. He lived as a man in relationship with His Father, who was His source. <u>He lived in relationship</u>. This is important because Jesus wants us to live in an atmosphere of love, faith, hope, and trust in the heart of the Father in heaven. This atmosphere in our own lives is cultivated and created by pursuing the heart of the Father in worshipful communion. That requires relationship and connection by waiting and spending time in His Holy Presence.

In God's word it says that we should become like Him in holiness and righteousness. He says to us: be holy because I AM holy. We grow in an understanding of holiness by entering into the heavenly throne room the God of Eternity, and by allowing Him to impact us with the greatness and awesome "otherness" that He is. We should desire to have a desire to become like Him, in His total "otherness." He is high and exalted; He is so holy. We are called to pursue Him and to be transformed into the image of His holiness. We need to be willing to sacrifice what we think pleasure is for the all-surpassing pleasure and holiness found in the love and authority of Jesus Christ. Jesus said that the Father desired that those who worship the Father would worship Him in spirit and in truth. Jesus says, essentially, that God loves worship that is based in the reality of who God is and what He is like. This, of course, transforms our life, but understand it is about God first. So it is vital that we as His people cultivate an attitude of worship. As you draw near to God and seek His face in worship and adoration, the presence of God will begin to transform more of your soul into the image of Jesus.

One of the gifts that we have received from God is the seal and mark of the Holy Spirit within us.

We received this gift by accepting and believing in the love of Jesus and His sacrifice on the cross on our behalf. We believe not only what we have read about His death, but also about His resurrection into glory. Because we believe, He pours into our hearts the love and presence and Spirit of God. You, as a disciple of Jesus, are called to new life and are given the ability to actually carry the spirit of resurrection power within you. Without exception this is the gift given to all believers in Jesus. Your human spirit, which was once darkened and without understanding, has been breathed upon and given resurrection life and the actual infusion of God! You have received this gift because of the complete authority and majesty of our Lord Jesus, and His victory over hell and darkness by dying on the cross as our sacrifice. He rose from the dead, and He has taken the keys to earth and hell and everything once for all. He has made your spirit alive and transformed you, and now joined your spirit with the Spirit of the one who created you. Put very simply: God lives on the inside of you NOW. Spirit to spirit, you are connected and filled.

So with that in mind I challenge you: do you know how to wait upon the Lord and access the heavenly realms like Jesus did? Jesus' primary relationship on the earth was not to parents, friends, disciples, or followers. His primary relationship was with His Father in heaven. Since Jesus is the model and He is the only one we seek to be like, we have to look at His relationship with the Father. He said, "The Son only does what He sees the Father doing." What does that sound like to you? Does it sound like He read a verse from the Old Testament whenever He was encountered by a demoniac, or a sick widow, or a dying child, or a violent storm, or starving people, or the Pharisees looking to trap Him, or His disciples asking Him a question? I do not see Jesus dependent on any book to get Him out of a jam or into a divine encounter. Jesus knew the written word, so don't discount knowing the written word of God. Please understand, I love the word of God, and I am not saying Jesus did not know the scriptures in His time. But He was and is the incarnate Word, so He is more important than the book, simply based upon His existence, since He is "The Word."

Jesus was in relationship with the Father, and the Father communicated with Jesus and led him by His Spirit. "Jesus was led by the Spirit into the desert," and it is reasonable to say that He was led through the earth by the Spirit as well. So when the Bible says in Psalms, "Where does our help come from?" the answer given is, "from the Lord who made heaven and earth." Where does our inspiration come from? It comes from above. Where does our individual calling and destiny come from? It should be from our communication with God. Our help and inspiration and call should be heard in a very real and tangible way, and it must be understood that this call is "from above." This is the kind of communication that Jesus showed us--right?

The problem is that most people do not function in actual one-on-one relationship with Jesus. They trust in the crutches of organizational religion, rather than learning to lean in total dependence on the Spirit of Jesus with no other option. If asked how we are called to communicate and listen to the Father, they would answer in theory but not in practice. Because of a severe lack of intimacy in relationship with God in today's church, the overwhelming experience and answer of the mainstream Christians is, "From a book right? The Bible, right?" Again, we need the word of God, but the Bible is NOT Jesus. (I say that because of the spirit of religious control and fear that seems to operate with a stranglehold on our hearts when we begin to talk about experience in God.) So many would say, our help comes only from a book because they come from a culture based on knowledge, where knowledge equals power. But first off we need to recognize that knowledge isn't our standard of authority in Jesus. Paul writes explicitly that knowledge puffs up, and that love builds up. Paul says that the love of God, the peace of God, and the spiritual expressions we share with God will transcend our natural mind or our wisdom and knowledge. The kingdom is not about academic knowledge. Man's knowledge is not equal to power as far as God is concerned. The power of God is true power in God's eyes. So our help is found in the Lord. Our relationship with Jesus, spirit to Spirit, is shown in the Bible and taught by Jesus in the Bible. But is our help from the Bible? Not exactly. It is supported and held in check by the Bible, without a doubt. Scripture is our standard. It is the guide. It is the backbone and test of our experience. Please hear me people, we read about Jesus in the Bible. But I believe that this generation's destiny and relationship to God, and to the world, is to be led by the Spirit of Jesus. Our help has always come from Father, Son, and Holy Spirit, but if we aren't careful, the spirit of religion will take over and we will believe our help comes from Father, Son, and Holy Bible, to the exclusion of the move of the Holy Spirit in our lives.

We, as disciples seeking real relationship and intimacy with the Father, cannot substitute the Spirit of Jesus for a book about Jesus. The written word is made to help us encounter the Living Word. Anything else will simply puff us up mentally, or make us more religious and arrogant because of knowledge of the word, not revelation from the word. The Holy Spirit' s instruction and communion as we read the word is our only hope of remaining humble and malleable before God, as well as compassionate and holy before God's created humankind. In thinking of Jesus' relationship with the Father, it is important to follow Jesus' words, and look at His lifestyle of going into the heavenly places with the Father. The Holy Spirit will lead us into the throne room of the Father where we receive wisdom, grace, favor and anything we need in our time of need. Each and every day you now have the right to approach the throne and see things from Heaven's perspective.

Personal Testimony:

I was in Washington D.C. at like 2:00 am with my friend and merch-guy extraordinaire, Colin the Terrible, and we were walking toward the Washington Monument. There was this rambling sidewalk that led up to the tower itself. The sense of connection and awe I felt as an American kid for his first time in D.C. was awesome, and really pretty satisfying in my heart. I was stoked to be there. We are walking towards the bright and tall monument when I became aware that we were walking across the grass. We were not aware of the rambling sidewalk until we were more than halfway there on our direct route to the base of the monument. I became aware of a "whoops" in my heart and felt like God spoke to my heart in that instant. He communicated to me something that I have kept with me when I think of our fear of coming before the Lord in the midst of our lives. It was like He said to me, in regards to coming before Him in the heavenlies, "This is how it is supposed to be when you come before me. Don't worry about man's protocol. Just get before me NOW! Just come right up. Don't take off your shoes, and don't be afraid of ruining the appearance of the place, just come to me as fast as you can! I am waiting. I love you. Come and sit in my lap and chill with me. I know it's awesome and impressive and scary and bigger than you will ever be, but I don't care about that more than I care about you. Come up. Don't worry about the sidewalk; it takes too long. Just get to me. Come on! Come on!!!"

We are dead in the flesh, and we are now seated with Jesus in heavenly places, so our home is, even right now, under the banner of eternal life, which starts on this side of eternity by the way. We have a responsibility to press into a heavenly calling and see what the Father is up to. We have the honor and right to become familiar with His presence and power and grace. We daily can worship Him and adore Him as the majestic King and Judge of all the earth. We worship and honor Him as the Father, believing on some level that through His love and our response, He can become the Father that the world would call out for if they could see Him. We must develop the relationship with the Father that Jesus had, doing only do what we see the Father doing. The Holy Spirit can escort us into heavenly encounters with the Father as we seek Him. We can grow in trust and learn to follow His Spirit into communion together as we live here, and live this as a lifestyle! What awesome and powerful realities we can walk in daily, realities on which we must fiercely maintain a hold. There is so much for us to taste and see in this current movement of God's Spirit on the earth.

Personal Testimony:

Sleeping Giant was on tour in Kentucky, and as we sat in the parking lot with a number of hardcore bands, we had a bible study about this very subject. I invited the Holy Spirit to show us whatever He wanted us to see, and to take us into heavenly places with Him if He wanted. Then we waited on God to do whatever. The presence and quiet of God was there. It was outside of a venue before the show started, and I was blown away that the cars and trucks driving sounded further away, and to me there was a feeling that where we were was becoming sacred space to the Lord because we were making space for Him to talk with us. After just literally like five minutes, we opened our eyes and I asked for anyone in the group to share what God had shown or communicated with them. There were a few seconds of trepidation and then my friend Manuel shared a picture that God gave him. Manuel thought he was making it up, but it revealed some things to him about his ability to see things and hear from God. Manuel had been embarrassed to share that he sometimes felt like he heard and saw things from God. He WAS embarrassed. But he began to cry when he realized that God loved him and talked with him, because he was a son of God.

Another member of a different band shared what he felt like God had shown him, then another member of another band shared, then another took their turn. In the midst of the testimonies we realized that one of our friends who had prayed with us was sitting there silent and couldn't open his eyes, tears were streaming out of the sides of his eyes. We began to get the feeling that God was up to something. Some of the Christian band members had never seen or been a part of any kind of prayer like this and were blown away. All we had done was to ask God to come and do whatever He wanted to do. As we all shared numerous things--from remembering old Bible stories in Sunday school that hadn't been thought of in ten years to seeing nothing, but feeling an overwhelming sense of peace for the first time in years--we realized that God was communicating to everyone in different ways. One of God's most favorite things to do is to connect with us in a way we understand and appreciate.

In the meantime, our friend, a guitarist from a notable Christian hardcore band, was stuck in his chair and couldn't move. He started to complain that he felt like his body was on fire, and asked us, was he really burning up? He was cold to the touch, and still couldn't open his eyes. Some of us who had seen God do this kind of thing were laughing in joy, knowing that God was touching this guy in a special way. Now understand this kid is not a charismatic kid. He came up in a super conservative church, and this kind of thing is unheard of for him and his denomination. However, I and some of the other dudes on tour at the time could tell that this guy had sensitivity to spiritual things, and it kind of made him react in a super religious way to a lot of this stuff. I was really honored that he came around and prayed with us. Really had he been standing up, he probably would have looked like he was in some Pentecostal meeting, and he would have fallen over. He was healed of a problem with his bladder, and he was able to physically see distances he hadn't been able to see, like his vision was impacted. He also had a vision of clouds parting and heaven's light shining on him. God physically healed him and showed him glorious things, and we had not even prayed for him. We just asked God to take us around heaven a bit and to show us some stuff that He could see.

This is not a pipedream, nor is it unbiblical or unscriptural. This is the reality of having a relationship with God and believing that God can and will communicate with you when you ask.

Exercise:

Have a heavenly encounter with your Father in heaven.

- Sit with your Bible and begin to look at John Chapter 14. Jesus begins to speak about his Father's house. Now this is romantic, Jewish wedding language stuff, but I want you to follow Jesus on this one.

- Begin to set an atmosphere of worship around you. Pray with gratitude for who God is to you. Give thanks for the sacrifice of Perfection for you.

- If you need worship music put it on. Create an atmosphere that is conducive for adoration to flow from your heart toward the Lord.

- Think about His goodness and majesty, His wisdom in sending Jesus, and His mercy in forgiving us. Begin to allow your heart and mind to be brought into submission to the Spirit of Jesus. Even pray that your soul, your mind, your will, and your emotions would be

brought into total submission to the Holy
Spirit on the inside of you. Give Jesus
authority over you in every way.

- Look at the Father's house with its many
  rooms. Jesus says, "I go there to prepare a
  place for you." Think about it for a minute
  and begin to ask the Lord, "Father, what does
  my room look like? What does your throne
  room look like?"

- Look at the Father in Revelation Chapters 4
  and 5. Look at the absolute limitless and
  endless worship and praise that goes up to
  God. Why? Because there is no other God
  like our God and Father of our Lord Jesus
  Christ. There is no other God like this God
  who is seated on the throne. Begin to declare
  to the Lord: "I must see you and I will see you
  and I will gaze upon your throne. Encounter
  me Jesus and take me to be with You."

- Ask the Holy Spirit to take you up to heaven
  to see the Father and to experience His heart.
  Now wait upon the Lord and give Him time to
  reveal things to you.

That's it.

If you begin to cultivate your secret life with Jesus, have an expectancy and reality around you that you have the right to see the Father NOW. You will contend and walk in a greater level of authority and understanding as his kid. Continue to press on even and especially if it is difficult to encounter God in these times. You have the right to visit with the Father anytime you wish. You will come to experience a greater sense of Jesus' presence and glory in your own heart and experience. This will translate in its time into you walking with a greater understanding of His presence with you each and every day. You were made to hang out with Jesus and experience His presence every moment. The atmosphere of heaven was Jesus' ally as He walked this earth, and He could see into the heavenly places. He had an understanding of what was really on the Father's heart. You can and will share in that revelation too.

You are destined to become and are in process now of becoming a revolutionary lover of Jesus, and you will see more of God than you thought possible as you pursue His love and His presence daily and hang out with Him in Heaven. It is that simple. You need to make the time for the exercise and practice. You have no need for fear or hesitancy. This is the kingdom we are destined for. Trust the Holy Spirit and the word of God to lead you into truth--spirit and truth. Become familiar with the atmosphere of heaven, and the presence of Jesus will be a compass and guide as you connect with God. You will find out what He requires of you each day. The atmosphere of heaven makes the impossible possible right before your eyes. One of the greatest miracles we experience daily is a relationship with the God of all Creation, who loves us enough to communicate with us each and every day. It is our honor to give God the time to communicate with us however He will. And it is our joy to obey and walk in relationship with Him each moment of our lives. The choice is yours. Engage with God today in the heavenly places.

Here ends the lesson.

Chapter 8.   Indigenous Style Warfare (a.k.a. Worship)

"I gave you life so you could live it."

The way I love GOD more is living life in honesty.

"Night and day, they never cease. . ."

"I plead with you to give you bodies to God because of all He has done for you. Let them be a living and holy sacrifice. . . . This is truly the way to worship Him."—Romans 12:1 (NLT)

The most dynamic and inclusive aspect of your Christian life is worship. Two things happen when you worship: you give a gift to God and you give a gift to yourself. Whether you choose to believe it or not, your life is a by-product of what you have given yourself. Also, your life is a gift, and your life was meant to be a gift given. In fact, it is with your life that you will worship God or you will worship something else. It is your choice.

Your life has value and it was meant to be given away, but only to those who can afford the price. There is only One who has paid the ultimate price for you; you are bought and paid for. You were meant to give your gift back to God by just existing in relationship with Him. Your life is meant to be a life of worship. You were created to worship.

Your human heart was given the most powerful ability in all of the universe--choice. Within the ability to choose you were given the ability to choose either life or death. A choice made generations ago still affects our life and existence. We walk out the choices of previous generations. We live under the weight of those consequences either unto something better than what was, or something worse than before. We are all aware that the choices we make affect more than just ourselves. Any one person or group who says, "it's my life it doesn't impact anybody else," is lying to themselves in an effort to alleviate responsibility for their own actions. Historically, we have seen the evidence that peoples and communities make decisions that affect larger groups and even larger groups, like the ripples that radiate from a stone dropped into a pond. That was the design. Biblically, no other creature was given the ability to make choices from a standpoint of the dominion and supremacy that would affect everything else through endless connections. We make choices and the world shakes under the impact. This is fact. Your choice makes choices for others. Your ability to make choices is the most precious gift you have ever received, and that ability has made you a powerful living entity. When you choose to give yourself to something, that choice can lead you into your destiny. Your destiny will either take you into deliverance or destruction. You choose. Choose.

We were designed to choose life. Our body screams out for life and our natural human chemistry is meant to exist in this life. When we experience a loss of life, we register it as something other than what we were designed to experience. There is a deep sense of loss when we lose a life. Why? Because we were made to live! Jesus said I have come that you may have life, and have it to the fullest. Not only were we destined to live, in God we were actually designed to live forever. Death was not part of the original plan. So now we live with the consequences of choices made so long ago.

When we choose to worship God in spirit and truth, we experience the transference from the kingdom of death, into the kingdom of His beloved Son, Jesus, which is the kingdom of eternal life. When you have been saved from death and brought into life, your heart has the ability to respond. You finally have the ability to give yourself to life. In making this choice, we create the opportunity to truly worship God. When humanity gives Jesus the authority He deserves over our destiny and lives, worship is birthed in that experience, and Jesus is given the glory for which the choice was given to us in the first place. This is our act of worship: a response to the fact that Jesus was punished for the brokenness and failure of all of us so that we could experience the true connection to the life within God. We stand in gratitude that starts in this life and will stretch out for all eternity, and we say, thank you Lord. That is worship. This is our reasonable response when someone loves us enough to die for us. We give them anything and everything they want for the sake of love and devotion.

The good news that should blow your mind is that all God wants for the life of His Son Jesus is your life--Now. Just say, "yes" and give Him the honor of being your Lord and Savior and King. Give Him the throne and rule over your life. Give Him a crown. The crown you give to Jesus is your own human love for Him. Volunteer to love Him. Make the choice to love Him forever and never look back towards the old way of life again. That's worship. Tell Him He can be in control, and then give Him control over your decisions for the rest of your days. This is worship. When you live with gratitude, honor, thanks, and faith in Jesus and His love for you, you are living in worship. When you live each day and for one brief moment you give him a gift-- telling Jesus, "I love you. You are the reason I want to live. You are my Lord today"--that's worship.

In the book of Revelation we see that God is seated on a throne and He is surrounded by living and breathing things. He is ultimately surrounded by the presence of adoration and worship directed to Him in an endless wave. Night and day, day and night, the creatures surrounding God declare how awesome and worthy and great the Lord is. So how does this translate to us in our daily lives? Well, first things first; our life is meant to be directed to God first. Then it's just a matter of logistics. How do we do it? I mean what does God really want from us in our everyday circumstances? How do we choose to choose?

God gave us all choice and he gave us all the ability to do different things. Psalm 139 tells us that who and what we are was designed and formed in the heart and mind of God before we ever showed up on the scene. When we give God a thank you for making us—for making YOU!--that's worship. When you allow God to get the credit for all of your "hard work and effort"--that's worship. When you use your ability to fix a car or paint a house or clean a floor or fix electronics or tutor someone in school, and in the midst of it you remember who put you here in the first place-- that's worship. When you stand with the homeless and down and out, and those suffering from injustice, and you raise God's banner on their behalf, and lift up your voice when they can't speak for themselves--that's worship. When you have kids and take care of them, and there is no one there to see what you go through, and you give a subtle and desperate, "God help me"-- that's worship. When you break inside and cry out in pain or frustration, all the while hoping that it will change or get better, and you ask God for help--that's worship. When you treat a friend like Jesus would treat a friend, even if they are acting like an enemy-- that's worship. When you listen to or create music that keeps or brings Jesus to mind, and you smile and say, "Hi Lord"--that's worship. When you get together with the saints and read the book of Jesus' life and times, and sing songs declaring how sweet God is, and then eat and make jokes and laugh--that is definitely worship. When you as a husband or wife make love together, knowing that God is as much a part of the bedroom as He is a part of the prayer room-- that's worship. And when you look into the eyes of your husband, wife children, family and friends and say, "I Love You"--that's worship.

Worship is not one size fits all. If you write or dance or tell stories, if you sing, sew, cook, serve, act, or love to read or hate to read, or like anything that brings your heart into connection with Jesus--this is the essence of worship. It is as unique and diverse as the people of God are. Worship is indigenous, it's tribal, and it fits any number of scenarios.

So as humans are given the ability to choose, God gives us the ability to choose Him in any number of ways that connect our life with His. That's worship. We cannot let the spirit of religion and fear-filled church control dictate to us what is and is not worship when the Bible states clearly, whatever you do whether in word or deed do it all in the name of Jesus. This is our indigenous-style warfare. That's freedom and that's choice. Will you waste your life on the nothings of this life, or will you give yourself to the God of worship who loves you so much and simply wants you to live with Him? Like the mama from the movie *My Big Fat Greek Wedding* said, "I gave you life, so you could <u>live</u> it."

This is our word from the Lord today and every day! **"LIVE life and thank Jesus Christ for the ability to waste your days on Him! You are free to Worship!"**

Exercises:

Sing, dance, paint, draw, hike, walk, run, play, write, create, tell jokes, laugh, eat, cook, serve, pray, preach, hang out, watch, contemplate, enjoy! Say to yourself, "When I _____ --that's worship." Fill in the blank yourself. It can all be worship!!!!

Chapter 9.   This Community is Bigger than You and Yours

To discuss true family and community in the kingdom of God makes our world a lot bigger. Tribal people we are, but kingdom we become.

"I pray also for those who believe in me through their message, that all of them may be one.   Father just as you are in Me and I am in You, may they also be in us SO THAT THE WORLD WILL KNOW THAT YOU SENT ME." –Jesus (John 17:20-21)

I love that the underground culture I'm a part of is very much its own tribe and culture. I LOVE IT. It is distinct, it is different, and it is special to me. I see aspects of true church in the scene that I have grown up and become a man within. The hardcore music scene can be full of politics and challenges, beefs and grudges, and trials and testing. It can be full of loyalty and true friendship, sacrifice for others, and real love and expression. It is a lens to view life, yourself, and the world around you.

There are aspects of "church" that need to be fostered within you, now that you have a new or existing relationship with Jesus. Your relationship with Jesus is the new lens through which you can view the community and body of Jesus, God, yourself, and others. Some of the values I have learned and appreciated about the hardcore scene and punk rock scene have stayed with me and have even grown as God has shown me what He valued about those same values. But my focus, now that I know God the way I do, is that God's view and expression of love to the earth is primarily to be my view. His view and expression is primarily meant to be expressed through His body, the church. That in mind it is important for anyone who is in relationship with Jesus to become a part of the greater community and body of Jesus. So if you aren't starting a community for those who don't have one, go find a community of people who love Jesus. Party with them until you love them and the rest of the body of Jesus in the earth, His church. SO, now I have some " 'splaining" to do.

There is practical wisdom in church community. In our new discipleship community, we become aware of the bigness of others and the smallness of our own ideas. We become more aware of the size and scope of the personalities and experiences of others, and we are given the opportunity to meet Jesus in every set of eyes we look into. The point of community is to express the desires in God's heart and personality through us all as community, while fulfilling that same desire in each one of us as individuals. That means that a singular would find a full expression as part of a corporate gathering, and that with others you would become a fuller expression of Jesus to the planet upon which you live. The biblical principle of our coming together is to form the body of Jesus as an expression of His person to the world, with Jesus rightly seated as the head. This is a great way to begin to talk about "church community" and why you cannot move forward in health without a spiritual determination and desire to overcome any and all offense. We walk in unity to display Jesus to the world that so desperately needs Him. We, as individuals in relationship with Jesus, will also get an opportunity to share in that experience of unity; we will see Jesus in new ways as we stand with the rest of "the body" in the earth.

I know that a majority of the people that I have spent my life with are not interested in looking like or being like a majority of the Christians they have met. So it is also a stretch for them to hang out with a group of people that has been labeled and may even have directly done some damage to them personally in relationship. So think of Jesus for a moment, and allow His grace to fill your mind. We have been forgiven and set free from all the stuff we have done before God. So now is the part where we honor the sacrifice and life of Jesus Christ, forgiving and releasing those who have hurt us in the church.

It is time for us to pray something like this:

"Jesus, I thank You that You have forgiven me for every time I have sinned and missed the mark. I know that You have forgiven me for everything that separated my life from Your life. I now declare and speak out that I forgive all of the Christians in my life who have hurt and offended me. I know they are not you, Jesus, and they are not perfect people. The things they did to me were not right, but I release them from any debt they owe me. I ask not only that You heal my heart from the pain I've experienced in the church or from church people, but I also ask that You would show me the "church" through Your eyes of grace and compassion. Do not allow me to hide any hatred or offense in my heart towards You in the form of Your body. Thank You for forgiveness and release from the hurt and anger. Please help me to be completely honest about harboring bitterness, and continue to heal my perspective and thoughts about Your people. I love You Jesus!"

So, moving forward, this is a principle I want you to understand as you read the summaries of these passages:

- Psalm 139 and Mark 12:28-- You have value as a person to the Lord, so others have that same value to the Lord. They should value you as well. This is the pursuit to love others with our whole self as part of the Greatest Commandment to love others as you love yourself.

- Matthew 25:40--You can see and encounter Jesus within the lives of others on the earth, so you need to stay open to others. Working for justice for the lowly, poor, and oppressed is also an important, healthy expression of Jesus to the world. When you can see Him in the dirty, dingy, underbelly of the world, you have touched His compassion and heart for those in need. This is real justice work: maintain the rights of the poor and oppressed.

- John 20:19-31, Acts 1-4 in general, but especially Acts 2:42-47-- When there is any form of governmental or legal persecution of people in the body of Jesus, the church is going to be functioning off the radar. Potentially our only option for support and community that will stand through trials with joy will be because of the Spirit of Jesus in our midst and within us all.

- Acts 4:32-37 and Psalm 133--Worship, unity, and support within the church, (the body of Christ, the brotherhood, the family of believers), is what Jesus wants and blesses. There is power and blessing when we stand together in love and we take care of one another, showing each other Jesus. Also we can break some of our own foolish consumerism and greed when we minister to the needs of our brothers and sisters.

This is important to me, personally: I am under the impression that the next generation of church planters and disciples are going to read this book, and I want you, as the underground and mainstream people, to have a healthy, deep respect and love for the rest of the church. That is the only way that kids coming up with no church background will have their hearts turned toward the fathers in the faith, so the fathers can have their hearts turned to the children. If the next generation of the church has a better-than-you-attitude toward their own brothers and sisters, then the church will stay jacked up and broken like everything else. Jesus wants us to walk in wholeness together. His prayer for us in Ephesians 3:16-19 is that we will all have power together to grasp how awesome His love is. WE CANNOT DO THIS ON OUR OWN. We need the rest of the church. We can't fight and mess each other up, or people are literally going to live and die in hell. It is our responsibility to love them as the body of Christ in the earth.

I speak this out clearly because I believe that this book can be used to help plant and build communities of faith in very unlikely places and I will not be responsible as a discipleship leader and pastor to allow the same rebellion and division that characterizes my whole life in the church. I cannot allow a generation to infect and divide the lives of people that Jesus died for and loves. I hope that's clear.

Essentially I am saying that you don't have to go to church where others go, or do what the rest of the body of Christ does, but you need to love and care for everyone who calls themselves a believer and follower of Jesus. No exceptions. Work that out with your time and life. In the meantime if you are open to the Holy Spirit, then you will remain a face of the body that will truly show Jesus to those in need, especially in the rest of the community of Christians around you. Whew. I have given you a lot to think about.

If you are starting a group and you don't have a church home, make sure you have connection with people in the greater community. Figure this thing out for yourselves. Remember: it is a journey of love for God and love for others.

Here ends the lesson.

Chapter 10. Noblesses Oblige: In Closing

The Honor Guard

The Accountability and letting go of yourself for the sake of the King, doing his name justice because of the relationship you have with eternity's King, the Unquestioned Judge, and Ruler of the Universe, the King of all Kings, the Name above all names—

Jesus Christ

Let your kingdom come.

You are all sons of God though faith in Christ Jesus.

All things are Yours.

One morning I was with my wife, Krissi, (my super hot wifey!), in the Boiler Room, which is the night and day prayer room we have set up at our church in Salt Lake City. I was legitimately pouring out to God some serious frustration and anguish that I had in my heart. I was pissed off and I was talking to God about it, basically. In the midst of my anger and emotion and just honest sadness, God interrupted me and said two things to me. First, he stopped me midsentence in the middle of my attempt to tell him that I show my love for Him through the things I do, but I felt so far away from my passion. Then God just said: "Thank You."

I lost my grip. I just broke down and started crying because of what was communicated to me, not just what He said, but what was communicated to my heart. More than a thank you, God expressed gratitude to ME. So crazy! All that I try to do for Him to show my love for Him and to honor Him and to help people meet my friend Jesus seemed so dumb, but HE CARED! That blesses my mind, you know?? It is so awesome that He really does care about me as a person and loves that I try. He spoke to me like a friend, you know, like He was saying, "Hey I get it. I see that there are areas where you are sad and broken about not being where you want to be, and you can't figure out what I'm doing with and through you. You are just feeling let down and tired. I get it. Can I just let you know something, Tommy? I see you and I am proud of your efforts. Thank You, kid!"

To hear God say that was awesome and it quieted my soul. I was able to just rest with Him in that place for a while. Then He spoke another two words to me and it sent me on a quest: "Honor Guard."

I am not in the military, and I didn't know what that meant so I called a dear friend of mine, Matt, who was a ranger in the military and served in Iraq multiple times because he is brave and sacrificial and an honorable gentleman. (Hi Matt.) I asked him about the words, "Honor Guard," and he explained them to me. Matt's explanation was the door to my understanding what God was communicating to me:

- The Honor Guard functions as the face and the representative of a movement or group to the public.

- Honor Guards may serve as ambassadors to the public, presenting a positive image of their service, and assisting with the recruiting effort. (That sounds like not only representing Jesus, but, as an evangelist, to bring people into relationship with Him.

I was excited about how that lined up with Jesus and me.)

- There are standards for those in the Honor Guard or Ceremonial Guard. Only those persons who are highly motivated and maintain exceptionally high standards of appearance and conduct, showing aptitude for ceremonial duty, are likely to be considered.

- They take their role seriously and believe in what they do. Their position matters, and their life, conduct, and walk is important.

- They are called "the chosen" and "the faithful."

I understand that I don't always act as a member of God's Honor Guard, but that is how God sees me. Matt's explanation was a gift, and it was an honor to hear that from him. I was truly broken open and wanted even more to make God proud as my Father and King and Lord.

This sounds so sweet, but it goes even deeper. God led me into a discussion about an obligation as a representative or ambassador to the world on His behalf. In Corinthians 2 and 5:20-21, we are called ambassadors for His kingdom. We are of royal blood now. The royal blood of Jesus now covers and leads us into sonship. We are sons and daughters of the King of All Kings. We are royalty in God's eyes.

This understanding led to the last part of this little word that God shared with me. There is a phrase that is expressed throughout history to define this mindset: Noblesse Oblige. Noblesse Oblige is the moral obligation of those of high birth or powerful social position to act with honor, kindness, and generosity. What it basically means is that with nobility comes a responsibility to act with nobility. Kings have an obligation to act as they are titled. With great power comes a great responsibility. "To whom much is entrusted, much is required." Awesome.

As royalty we have an obligation to act accordingly. Paul says it like this "We have an obligation now, not to the sinful nature, but to the

Spirit of God, to keep in step with the Spirit, not following our old sinful desires." We are co-heirs with Jesus Christ now. We get the same treatment as Jesus did from the Father and we share in an inheritance together now! God sees us and loves us and honors us like He honors Jesus!!!!

We have been changed spiritually now that we have come to accept the sacrifice on our behalf and Spirit of Christ. We are now royal blood. We are sons and kings and priests in a kingdom that has no end. We are victorious! We have <u>everything</u> now.

So there is a sacred and holy responsibility because of our relationship with the King. We are called to be royalty and to live accordingly. This is a principle that God has been showing me, and it is a lifetime revelation that will continue to unfold in all areas of my life. I believe it is fitting and appropriate to release it to you, that you would begin to walk in the royalty of Jesus and share it with those around you. As a son of the King you have at your disposal all the resources of heaven. You have a place and destiny that is rooted and grounded in the unconditional love of Jesus for you, and you have a standing and open daily invitation into the throne room of God. There you can receive from your Father in Heaven wisdom and understanding, as well as strategies and resources for your times of need. Not only will you receive help for yourself, but also for the world around you. You are chosen and set apart for a divine and amazing life in the family of God and you do not have to settle for some cookie-cutter Christian experience for the rest of your days. The God I know is alive as an all consuming fire, and His children are designed to be filled and consumed with the fire of His love. Again, our Father has given us a new life to live. The tools and resources that have been laid in front of you are there and available. Go hard after this relationship you have with Jesus. It is the only true and lasting way of life you will ever find. Do it because God has given you a new place in human history as part of a royal family, an honored one in the halls of heaven.

Walk in faith and persevere even when things are tough and life is difficult to manage. Put your whole life in the hands of your Father in heaven who loves you so much, He sacrificed His only Son for you. You are the Honor Guard in the kingdom. You are the face of the church. You are kings and priests. You are children of the Most High God. You are eternal and unbreakable now because of Jesus alive in you. You have it all. Live it up and honor the King who died for you. Die to what you thought you knew and be reborn in the Spirit of the Lord <u>every single day</u>.

Above everything else, live for love. Experience and drink deep from the love of God and live in that place of divine and royal love. Noblesse Oblige. . .

I pray the grace of Jesus Christ would rest upon your every action and reaction for the rest of your days, and that you would have the life of Jesus, the faith of Jesus, the joy of Jesus, the fellowship of Jesus, and the sufferings of Jesus in your own experience. I pray that He would be the most important love you will ever pursue with all that you are and all you hope to become.

This is your life and your journey. Go with God, and let His Kingdom come. Do not settle for the systems of controls and religious manipulation when all of Jesus is available to you. You are the Honor Guard. Remember Now. Remember Him.

Noblesse Oblige. . .

Here ends the lesson.

Recommended Reading:

The Holy Bible

Recommended Resources:

Brother Andrew, Rob Bell, Mike Bickle, Shawn Bolz, George Bowker, Nicky Cruz, John Eldredge, Sean Feucht & Andy Byrd, Billy Graham, Eric Gregson, Pete Greig & Dave Roberts, Jack Hayford, Bill Johnson, Martha Kilpatrick, John G. Lake, Jaeson Ma, Brennan Manning, Josh McDowell, Tim and Cindy McGill (write your books!), Donald Miller, Watchman Nee, Leonard Ravenhill, Lee Stroebel, A. W. Tozer, David Wilkerson, Mike Yaconelli

Made in the USA
Charleston, SC
31 January 2011